Moving Aw

THE EMOTIONAL SIDE OF LEAVING

By: Brooke Baum

Published by: Next Step Editing

Copyright © 2020 Brooke Baum All Rights Reserved

No part of this publication may be reproduced, distributed, or transmitted in any form or by any means, including photocopying, recording, or other electronic or mechanical methods, or by any information storage and retrieval system without the prior written permission of the publisher, except in the case of very brief quotations embodied in critical reviews and certain other noncommercial uses permitted by copyright law.

Legal Notice:

Please note that much of this publication is based on personal experience. Although the author and publisher have made every reasonable attempt to achieve complete accuracy of the content in this product, they assume no responsibility for errors or omissions.

The author is also not a financial advisor or mental health professional. This book is for informational purposes only and the views expressed are personal opinions offered to the reader for the purpose of inspiring and encouraging. If you need additional support, you should seek out a professional for psychological, relationship, and/or financial advice.

Author:

Brooke Baum
TrailingAway.com

Table of Contents

1 Introduction

7 Why Move Away?

23 Addressing the Guilt

33 Dealing with Resentments

47 How Relationships Change

59 Harsh Realities of a Life Away

69 Being Scared & Doing It Anyway

79 Becoming Yourself

87 Building Stronger Bonds as a Couple

97 Being Far Away & Nomad Insights

109 Final Thoughts

112 Before You Go: Practical Checklists

Acknowledgements

About the Author

Introduction

There's nothing quite like a worldwide pandemic to make you reassess all of your major life choices. As my husband and I scrambled to find a temporary home in New Zealand – half a world and an entire day away from our loved ones in the U.S. – the realities of living so far from our extended support system really hit us harder than usual.

At first, we felt very alone and scared. We worried about when we would see our family and friends again. We desperately wanted to be surrounded by people who would take us in and make sure we were safe. But, after a few hours of feeling sorry for ourselves, we shook it off, looked in the mirror, and reminded ourselves that is not the life we signed up for.

We put our hometown in our rearview all those years ago to find out who we really are, form our own opinions, and lean into our marriage as well as our own personal growth.

When we left, it was actually really easy. We didn't feel very connected to many people in our lives at the time (aside from a precious toddler nephew, of course!). There wasn't much capturing our interests or exciting goals to work toward. Our future in that city just seemed dull.

While most of those things are still true about our hometown, the reason I wanted to hug my people so badly during this crisis is because having space and time away from them allowed us to heal our relationships and stop taking each other for granted.

We DO feel connected to so many more people now. That's not everyone's moving away story, but the phrase "absence makes the heart grow fonder" is popular for a reason – it's often very true.

It has been almost a decade since we left our hometown in North Florida. Since then, we spent five years living in Colorado, then left to try out RV life, and finally traded our rolling home in for backpacks to travel the world as house and pet sitters. We've moved often in our life together and have experienced that feeling of sadness-tinged excitement each time we leave to make a new home.

With our tendency to move again and again, then return to places we once called home just to leave soon after, we are constantly in the process of making, maintaining, and letting go of relationships. Saying it is complicated is a vast understatement.

The purpose of sharing my experiences and epiphanies in this book is to let others know it's okay to be scared, sad, excited, confused, or relieved to leave your hometown, chosen home, or even entire country for a new adventure.

Moving away brings on a lot of emotions and they will continue to change along with your view of the world.

Going home to visit may be a chore at first, but may later become a welcome tradition. You may return a much different person than when you originally left. Or you might even decide to move back.

While others will choose to move even further (spoiler: US!). It's your choice. And that's the beauty of it.

A few years ago, I wrote a blog post titled *"Why You're Not Selfish for Moving Away"* for the website where my husband and I share our travels, and it has been the single most popular piece of content I've ever written.

While moving to a new place may seem simple on paper, it is very emotionally charged for many – especially if they are the first to leave home or their family is against it.

I get messages almost weekly from people who feel like they finally found someone who understands their struggles.

While the messages can be heartbreaking, it has also been an absolute joy to know my words can bring another human even a little bit of peace during a difficult life adjustment or inspire someone to chase their dreams. I've laughed, cried, and nodded along as I read these heartfelt notes that are all too relatable.

However, I only touched the tip of the iceberg in that blog post and have so much more to share. I've gained many valuable lessons about moving away and experienced many versions of it. So, I wanted to put together a more complete guide – an outpouring of all my insights – for anyone who is struggling with the decision to move, has already left and wants to know they aren't alone in their feelings, or for those who want to better understand what this decision may be like for loved ones.

I know that this big life transition can feel lonely and overwhelming at times, but please know you are not alone.

And it WILL get better, but it will also take some work ... and time.

What they don't tell you about chasing your dreams is that it may be the most difficult thing you do. But, in my case – and for many others I've connected with, it has also been the BEST decision.

Questions to Ask Yourself

Before we get started, take a few minutes to answer or contemplate these questions.

Why do (or did) I want to move away?

What am I struggling with most about it?

What benefits will I gain from my move?

What fears do I have about moving away?

How do I think my relationships might change?

Why Move Away?

One of the biggest questions you'll receive when sharing your decision to move will be 'why?'

Whether that's to the tune of, "Why would you leave this awesome place?" or "Why would you go so far away from me?" or "Why would you go through that hassle?"

For people who have never moved, it can be a strange concept to wrap their head around. For the person moving, it feels like your life choices are constantly being critically questioned – even if most people are just being curious.

It's often a challenge for everyone involved, especially in a country like America where people tend to stay put.

According to the 2018 U.S. Census Bureau Data, only about 14% of Americans moved away in the year prior. Of those, 7.9% moved within their own county, 3.3% moved out of the county but stayed in the same state, and just 2.3% moved to a different state.

I'm not usually one to geek out over data, but I was curious about finding more information on the topic of moving away and these statistics kind of blew my mind.

While I already knew moving wasn't extremely common in the U.S., I had no idea it was this unlikely.

No wonder moving away feels like uncharted territory as an American ... it is!

While the U.S. census data does not include information on people who left the country, I can only guess that it is an even smaller number.

Strangely, the percentage of people to move away has actually been mostly trending DOWN since the 1940s. With the ease of travel, remote work, and technologies that make it much simpler to keep in touch, you would think more people would start to consider the benefits of moving away.

But even if that does happen, it will likely never be the go-to life plan of Americans in the foreseeable future.

Of course, the trends around choosing to move away likely differ in other countries. However, I'd be willing to bet that even in areas where planning a move to a new area or emigrating to an entirely new country is much more common, those who move away often still feel a confusing mix of emotions. (Granted, I do acknowledge that being able to *choose* to move is a luxury in itself that not everyone has).

For some people who decide to move, they may be the first in generations to leave or the only person they know. Perhaps the ones who stay never even considered moving because it is so uncommon or maybe they just love the place they live and are genuinely happy there. Or it could be that financial, work, family, or personal circumstances are preventing them from going elsewhere.

Moving to pursue a college degree somewhere else is one of the most common reasons for leaving your hometown in the U.S. – with more than 6% of people aged 18-19 moving out of state (the highest of all age brackets).

In many other countries, a 'gap year' of travel after primary school is standard and even encouraged as an opportunity to gain self-reliance and an expanded perspective on life.

That's not often the case in the U.S., but some young people do use going to university as an opportunity to expand their horizons and experience a new place. On occasion, they will love it so much that they won't return home.

We've also met plenty of people who moved simply to be in a climate they enjoy better or to be with a spouse who they met outside of their hometown – or even country. For some couples, there is a desire to want to start your own journey and go somewhere new where you can make your own traditions and unique life, or offer new opportunities to current or future children.

Then, of course, there are the ones who are looking for an escape from family drama, politics, location-specific issues, or a fresh start after personal trauma.

But for others, like us, there are no outside forces pulling you to a new destination or big issues pushing you away. No big reason to point to when the move is questioned. Words like boredom or restlessness are thrown around, but those don't quite explain the yearning.

For some, the decision to move comes from an internal desire to leave – whether to pursue a dream of travel or find a more preferred way of life. Or maybe because you just crave a change of scenery and can't quite explain why.

If you feel this way, you know exactly the pull I'm talking about. And if you don't, it is probably really difficult to understand why loved ones, stability, and familiarity aren't enough to keep someone in one place.

But that's okay. To be honest, it's actually really difficult for me to relate to the idea of wanting to stay put and never having a desire to see far-off places.

In the same way people have asked me why I moved, I find myself wanting to reply, "But aren't you curious what else is out there?" or "Don't you want to be challenged by new experiences?"

However, as I've gotten older, I've learned to just respect that everyone finds happiness in different ways – not everyone needs to go searching for it. But for those of us who do, it can be a challenge to try to explain why it feels that our true self is waiting in some far-off place.

Out of the already small percentage of people who move away, those of us who leave for the sheer sake of going are probably the biggest outliers.

OUR MOVING AWAY STORY

Personally, I never remember a time I didn't want to move away from my hometown. As soon as I learned there were far-off lands to be explored and different ways of doing life, I wanted to experience that for myself.

~~I was chronically bored as a child and young adult~~ with all my spare time dedicated to dreaming of exciting places to go. So many people love vacationing in Florida for the beaches and theme parks, but I wasn't impressed. I guess some people just have a natural curiosity for new experiences and I always remember having that.

Plus, let's be real. Florida is filled with snakes, bugs, hurricanes, and a lack of seasons. Our hometown also had a severe lack of jobs at the time, felt very materialistic for us nature-lovers, had an intense drinking culture we didn't partake in, and everyone we knew spent weekends watching sports or going to the beach – neither of which we cared about.

Of course, falling in love and marrying someone with the same unquenchable desire for novelty and excitement (and hometown hatred) meant we were destined to leave. Especially because we both come from divorced families with no real sense of 'home' to keep us tethered.

Not long after getting married, my husband Buddy and I took off with just a car packed to the brim and giant smiles. I don't even remember crying when we started out on our cross-country move. The entire exhausting drive was just filled with excitement and hope and a deep pride in being brave enough to go for it – despite everyone who didn't like our decision.

While our first chosen home of Colorado still had some of the things we didn't love about Florida – like snakes – it also had mountains and trails and snow and recycling, plus fun start-up companies and people with different outlooks on life. And, most importantly, it had that amazing feeling of newness an unfamiliar place holds.

We couldn't wait to get there and were smitten every day we spent living there. I'd smile a gracious grin every day when I saw those mountains because they represented the promise of adventure in our new home.

The only person I really had a hard time saying goodbye to in Florida was our nephew who was only three at the time. Sure, there were other people we'd miss, but phone calls would do just fine with them! We were extremely close to that adorable little dude and missing out on watching him grow was (and still is) the most painful part of moving away for me.

To be completely honest, if my nephew hadn't come into our lives, we likely would have left much sooner. It was just always the plan since we met. Get out of this dead-end town!

As much as I cherished my time with him, I couldn't find a way to pursue the person I wanted to be and stay close by. Although difficult, we knew it was the right choice as soon as we fully committed to moving.

I'll never forget the day we officially decided to leave. We had honeymooned in Colorado and knew it was where we were meant to be, but after working for almost a year to try to get job transfers out there, the paperwork just kept getting held up.

So, as we were picking out some cheese to go with dinner, I had this epiphany about it. Out of nowhere, I looked at Buddy and asked, *"why don't we just go anyway?"*

Within three months of that day, we were on our way – with nothing very certain to lean on except a strong faith that it would all work out. And we also packed about 15 peanut butter and jelly sandwiches to bring along for the drive ... just to be safe.

For us, moving to Colorado very much meant choosing love, and the excitement, challenges, surprises, and joy that come with a good love story.

It was loving ourselves enough to do what was best for our spirits and marriage. And loving our friends and family enough to know the miles would never change our feelings for them.

IMPORTANT NOTES ON MOVING AWAY

However, it is important to note that **we had already done our research before abruptly deciding to go for our big move.** We knew how much it would cost to move, what areas we could live in, possible job opportunities, and that a life in Colorado was indeed feasible for us.

We had enough money saved up to float us for a little while and the blind determination needed to overcome any obstacle. Besides, if we failed miserably, we could always go back to our hometown and ask family for help (never our style, but always an option).

I also think it is worth mentioning that **we never ask for outside opinions on these kinds of decisions**. We may get tips from someone who has insights in the area we want to move to or with similar experiences, but we don't invite anyone else – especially family – to chime in on our big decisions.

It's not that we don't value these relationships, it's that we have very different life goals and perspectives. Asking for people who aren't on the same page to speak into our plans, just isn't practical.

We discussed our move in secret, made a plan, then told everyone what we were doing. A lot of people were sad, some even told us we'd move right back. But their opinions never changed our determination to move because they were never invited to speak into our lives in that way.

I know people who are much closer to their parents or siblings who need their approval on every big decision, but that just isn't how we live. And I think it makes big things like this so much easier.

There's something very different about telling someone about your plans with confidence versus asking them with uncertainty to weigh in. I think this actually helps loved ones feel better about the move because your excitement and certainty can put them more at ease. Not acting like moving makes you guilty of some betrayal is also helpful to not invite that kind of criticism.

You can acknowledge and be empathetic toward their feelings of sadness or disappointment without having to feel sorry for pursuing something else or diminish how much you are looking forward to your new adventure.

A lot of people struggle to give an unbiased opinion, so of course, some loved ones will try to make you stay out of an understandable personal desire to have you close. However, we've found that a happy medium is possible!

Our best supporters are the ones who are sad to see us go but smile for us anyway because they know we are chasing our dreams.

WHY MULTIPLE MOVES IS OKAY, TOO!

While moving away from our hometown in Florida was certainly the first extremely impactful move we've made, it wasn't our last. Spontaneous changes in our home base have actually become a bit of a theme for us.

One of us asks a big, life-changing, cataclysmic question and, before we know it, the course of our life has changed again with not much more than faith and a sense of adventure guiding us.

We've always tried to be hyper-focused on prioritizing what is best for our marriage and sometimes a change of scenery is exactly what we need to refocus. We feel moving to a new place or taking on a completely new lifestyle offers a change in perspective and new challenges to bring us closer together and inspire us individually.

However, moving can still be difficult even if it is from a place where you've only lived for a few years. When we left Colorado, it was much harder than leaving our hometown in Florida. Part of me felt like I could be making a huge mistake.

I felt guilty for getting exactly what I always wanted, then deciding I wanted even more out of life. But the louder voice was saying, *'You've gotten what you needed here, time to move on.'*

I really had to sit with my feelings a lot and mourn what we were leaving behind – a chosen home that was so very good to us for five years, amazing friends who loved us dearly, and a very stable, traditionally successful life.

But even with all the beautiful nature, we had gotten caught up in the materialism and workaholic nonsense we always hated, so a drastic change felt mandatory to shake us out of it. And a year in a motorhome definitely did the trick.

The point is, it is okay if it takes a few tries before you find the right place. It's okay if a place you love doesn't fit your needs anymore. Or even if you end up moving back to that hometown you were so desperate to leave. None of that is failure.

There is no right way when it comes to making a life for yourself. It's a lot of trial and error, chasing curiosities, backtracking at times, then making a new plan.

Sometimes you get to be in control of your path and sometimes outside forces push you in a certain direction (like a lost job, sick loved one, personal diagnosis, pandemic, etc.). All you can do is try your best to ride the waves and angle yourself in the right direction.

THE IMPORTANCE OF PLACE

While sometimes you just feel the need to move ANYWHERE new. A lot of times, there is a special place in mind that you've visited or heard of that sounds like an ideal fit for the kind of life you want.

Certain places just light up your soul. I've felt God in the still, crisp mountain air of Colorado and in the breeze tickling a sunset-lit ocean in Greece. Although we've found that it is up to us to bring that sense of home with us, there is no denying that certain places just have a little more to offer.

For us, we find the most joy and peace in outdoor-focused areas, far from cities and with wildlife dotting the scenic views. We feel at home near nature. And if the weather is nice, then we're more likely to want to stay longer.

Although we love seasons, we've found that we really shut down and lose motivation in the depths of winter. We eat too much, stop exercising, and get really lazy. We just don't like the hassle of going out in the cold. So, when considering our next long-term home, the weather weighs heavily on our minds.

We have also realized that food, people, and culture are all extremely important factors to us. I desperately wanted to have a desire to move to Germany when we visited, since that was where my grandma was from, but I just didn't feel the connection. It's a lovely place, but with a very success-and rule-oriented culture with very meat-focused dishes. It just wasn't a long-term home option for us.

I'm sure you know in your heart what draws you to a place – or pushes you away – as well.

However, that being said, even in the most unideal places, we've found a way to make a sense of home. While certain places mesh with our personalities and preferences more, we can find a way to get comfortable in almost any situation – some just take more adjustments than others!

The best part about travel, to us, is the ability to imagine what life as a local in a new place would be like and try it out for a time. Things like grocery shopping, going out to eat, chatting with locals while out walking, and taking public transport or driving all become little mini-adventures. We love it!

If you aren't sure where you may want to move, spending some time traveling to different places can be a great help at narrowing it down, if you are able to do that.

We have friends who spent a year RVing all around the U.S. in order to decide where they wanted to move. And we have plenty of fellow housesitting friends who have used housesitting as a way to test out lives in new cities or countries before committing to a permanent move. It's always nice to be able to test the waters!

AVOIDING SHINY PLACE SYNDROME

However, we are fully aware that the ability to follow a dream and see where it leads is an immense privilege. Not ever having to look back and wonder, *what if?* ... that's something not many people can do.

Yet, at the same time, there is something to be said about being happy where you are and not getting in the habit of always looking for the next best thing. Of course, new adventures are exciting and offer this shiny, tempting image of an even better existence. But, be realistic. No location is perfect.

Sometimes a big, dramatic move isn't what you really need.

Sometimes it is a different major life adjustment or a smaller move to a more relaxing rural area or somewhere that would decrease the commute you hate.

It's taken us three years of full-time travel after leaving Colorado to realize all we've really ever wanted is a simple life not dominated by working for other people, plus lots of time outside and some fun adventures scattered in. We probably didn't need to cross the country in an RV and travel the world to figure that out, but we certainly don't regret it.

Sure, we've spent far more money than we needed to and made a ton of poorly planned decisions along the way. But, what a story we have now!

It was uncomfortable a lot and has really pushed us in ways we would have rather not been at times. But looking back, we needed it to figure out what we wanted out of life.

However, every story is different and what one person has to endure to change, others could just read about and take in another person's insights or overcome in some other way.

Just know that no matter what path in life you choose, there will be challenges. Struggles will arise whether you stay or go. No matter how far away you are or how close to your hometown you remain, life still happens. You still experience all the good and bad. You'll have successes. You'll make mistakes.

So, please, just cut yourself a break as you search for what 'home' really looks like to you. Whether that adventure takes you a short drive away or to the other side of the world, enjoy the experiences along the way.

Questions to Ask Yourself

Did something specific trigger your desire to move away?

If you are staying at the moment, is it for your own reasons or someone else's?

What are some of the things you actually like about your life right now?

What are you wanting that you aren't getting in your current location?

Could you make any adjustments to be happy without moving?

Do you have an ideal place you'd like to move, and will it provide what you are missing?

Addressing the Guilt

Even when you are sure of your decision, moving away from the people you love is still an exercise in faith. You believe you'll see them again. You believe your love is strong enough to bridge the distance. But you just aren't sure you will be able to get through it until you make the leap.

For us, moving away has solidified which people are the most important to us and vice versa. It becomes obvious quickly that you're not a priority if the calls and visits and letters are all one-way.

There have been times when we've been back in town and a friend can't be bothered to meet us around the corner from their house or lock in a time for us to swing by. So disappointing!

But, really, it isn't the people who don't value your relationship that will pull on your heartstrings. You may cry a few tears for those lost connections, but eventually, they will be a memory.

It's the people who do make an effort ... who tell you they miss you all the time, call to check in regularly, can't wait to plan their visit, block out their whole week to spend time with you when you are back, run to hug you when you arrive, cry when it's time to say goodbye. Those are the people who will make it hard to move away and who you will feel painfully guilty for leaving – especially during special occasions and even more so at hard times.

It can make you feel extremely selfish to know you chose a life that removed you from them in a way that makes showing up more challenging – or in some situations, impossible.

WHY THE LITTLEST PEOPLE CAUSE MORE GUILT

My nephew has always been one of those people for me who I just miss daily and hate not getting to see more often. As he gets older, I have realized my postcards and once or twice a year visits probably don't make as much of an impact.

He's a pre-teen now. (*Ugh! Just writing that is a jab in my heart!*) I know, without a doubt that he'd benefit so much from weekly Auntie dates and gaming time or life advice from his goofy Uncle. We try to call often and encourage him to do the same, but he says "*I don't want to bother you*" because he knows we are off traveling somewhere.

It doesn't matter how many times I tell him he is a top priority. We aren't there. We left. He doesn't get it yet. I hope maybe one day he does, and it inspires him to follow his own dreams. But it's hard right now and probably will be for a while.

I remember him being our entire world for the first three years of his life before we moved. But ... he doesn't.

I remember using up all of my vacation time from my desk job and spending hundreds of dollars to be able to spend his spring break with him or surprise him for his birthday. But those are distant memories for him when it has been months since we've laughed together.

Plus, recent trips back have been focused on weddings and new babies and much-needed friend time I crave when off traveling. While I cherish that time with other loved ones, it does take away from giving him the days of one-on-one time I'd like to.

And, to be really honest, I'm not all that sure how to connect with him as a non-video gamer (his most favorite thing to do these days). I feel like I'm just pulling him away from something more fun at times. Granted, I still find creative ways for us to have fun together. But it is challenging, especially for a chronic over-thinker!

It just sucks to feel so disconnected. I make excuses, but deep down I feel like I've failed him for not being there more often and in more meaningful ways. Maybe I'd be better at coming up with fun things to do with him or talk to him about if I didn't miss huge chunks of his childhood. Maybe I'd be the one he calls when he is having a bad day if I was around the corner and could meet for a walk or ice cream.

It really breaks my heart to not be closer. And now that we have other little ones in our life as well, there are even more strings of my heart being pulled! I feel especially awful when something is going on I want to be around to offer in-person support for.

IT IS NOT ALL ON YOU

There have been times where the guilt of being so physically far away has actually made me consider moving back – especially when there have been really hard times for my family. I just wanted to be there to help in any way I could and offer ongoing, reliable support. We've really agonized over it on a few occasions.

I just kept going over it again and again in my head ... Would our presence even help, or would we just antagonize the situation? Would I be able to suck it up and be happy to be there even though I deeply dislike that boring city? Would my marriage suffer? Was I just being overly self-absorbed to think we were the ones who could swoop in and save everyone?

Of course, giving up your personal desires to selflessly help someone you love is a beautiful thing. But the truth is, aside from diagnosis and other unfortunate circumstances, most people in your life will get along just fine without you.

I'm sure I'm not the only one who likes to think of myself as the important glue that can hold the people I love together.

Sure, my help would be welcomed and appreciated. (And sometimes it makes sense to go back for a longer period to help). But, it's not up to me to fix their lives for them in some unhealthy co-dependent way.

Realistically, there is only so much we can do. Eventually, everyone goes back to their routine and we are left feeling unsure of where we belong again. At that point, we're offering the same level of support we could from the phone in a place we feel more at peace.

Had I stayed or moved back, I wouldn't be the person I am today that is able to offer the level of emotional support to my loved ones that I can. It would have felt like a burden rather than a gift to be able to step up for the people I love when they need me.

It is really hard to wonder if I could have prevented some of the pain and loss. But who knows ... had I stayed, maybe I would have meddled and made things worse for the people in my life because I was so dang bored in that city, what the hell else was there to do?!? Maybe I'd be the one struggling the most...

Deep down, I realized part of me just wants to be the one to fix the problems. I want to be needed. I want to be valued. I think that's how I feel most connected and validated. But this experience of moving away has made me realize there is so much more to relationships than that.

Not only have I grown into a better person, noticing the people I love getting empowered to take charge of their own lives has been much more meaningful than just holding their hand along the way. Of course, I am happy to offer support and encouragement, but in a healthy way – not just trying to fix it for them. And finding my value in being loved for who I am and not just the help I can offer, has been life-changing.

THEY MAY NOT ACTUALLY NEED YOU

It's funny really, you spend all this time feeling bad about moving away, missing out on things, and not being there in person for loved ones. Then you return for a visit and realize they've gotten along just fine. Sure, they miss you. Sure, you probably could have helped them on multiple occasions. But, at least in our experience, their world went on remotely the same as it would have if you had been there. Maybe even better!

That's because, for most of us, living at home meant a weekly meal with loved ones max , and often we'd go more than a month without seeing them because we all have life stuff that takes priority – jobs, spouses, kids, school, hobbies, fitness ... the list goes on.

The main thing that really changes when you move away is you – your entire life. So, it feels immensely different. But, to them, it's often just your proximity.

The hard truth is: Your loved ones will likely make do just fine without you. It may be a jab to your ego, but they probably don't *really* need you as much as you think or they may say they do.

They may want you there desperately, but somehow they will figure out a way to do life without your in-person help and good company. Because they have to.

And, to be extremely direct, *could that be exactly what some people in your life need? A little less hand-holding? A little more distance and boundaries?*

It's hard to realize you aren't needed. But the other side of that is realizing that you are VALUED for more than just the help you can provide. When we go back to visit, we aren't (*usually*) the babysitter or the errand runner or the emergency call. We're the ones they want to hug and spend hours chatting with and make lasting memories with.

Because the people we love, actually LIKE us a whole lot too. Wow! *Could you even imagine?!?* And moving away allowed us to really acknowledge that.

There is this idea some people have that because you aren't close by, you will no longer be "close" in heart in the same way either. But that second part just isn't true. You can still be there for your loved ones without, well ... being there.

Most issues would probably be discussed over a phone call no matter if you are up the road or on another continent. Of course, emergencies happen, but that shouldn't be a weekly or even yearly occurrence with most relationships!

Sitting around in a place that you can't stand, "just in case" you're needed in person is a recipe for resentment.

You may actually be surprised to find out how well most people get along without you there! And if you do have a parent or family member that genuinely needs your assistance, maybe it would be worth it to figure out a way for all of you to move, if that's a dream you want to pursue.

While feeling guilty or selfish for moving away is common, it is important to remember those are *feelings,* not *facts*. Actual guilt is the result of doing something wrong. Actual selfishness is not considering others.

People you love may not understand why you are moving and may become angry or sad when they hear the news, but the way you act makes all the difference.

Don't give yourself anything to be guilty for, try to be empathetic, and leave on good terms if at all possible. It will make such a positive impact!

Questions to Ask Yourself

Who are the most important people in your life?

Would they be excited for you to follow your dreams?

By moving, would you actually be doing anything wrong to feel guilty about?

Do you show up for them in important ways, no matter how far you are?

Are you giving yourself an unrealistic level of importance in other people's lives?

Would they want you to feel guilty? What would they say to you about it?

Dealing with Resentments

Unfortunately, not all unwarranted guilt is self-inflicted and can be dealt with through personal reflection. Sometimes guilt is shoved down your throat in a hateful way. Sometimes the people you love most resent you for wanting to move and try to use guilt as a way to sway you to stay.

But if you let them coerce you, there's a high chance you'll be the one who ends up being resentful. It's a really tough situation.

For couples with children, we've been told that taking the grandchildren away can become an especially big point of contention in families. Even though many parents are just pursuing a life they think would be better and more aligned with the future they want for themselves and their kids, the grandparents can let the idea of missing time with those precious little ones send them into a fit of blind anger.

On the other hand, we've talked to retirees who decided to take off on their dream to travel or move to a different place (often after spending decades raising a family), who are met with angry adult children who feel like they are being abandoned.

It's hard to see that kind of resentment coming and deal with it in a productive way when you are excited to pursue a personal dream you've been yearning for, especially if you were actually expecting your happiness to be reflected!

We are extremely fortunate to have family and friends who have supported us overall – even in our craziest of adventures. They worry, they don't get it, a few make negative comments ... but if they see that we are happy, they are usually happy for us as well.

However, we've had some people reach out to us with horrific stories about family who are trying to shame them into staying nearby because they can't bear to see them go.

Sometimes they go so far as to make threats to basically disown the person leaving or become verbally abusive or manipulative in other ways.

These family members claim to love them too much to be able to live without them. They say the person who is planning to move is just being selfish. But to us, that's just not love.

And it is a whole lot more selfish for people who claim to love you to try to prevent you from living out your dreams just for the comfort of knowing you're close. Of course, most people won't see it that way since it is often disguised with words of love. But it is definitely self-motivated.

If you stay because you are trying to appease someone else, you can easily become bitter toward a life you feel you are settling for, especially when we live in a world where there are so many other possible options.

It seems awful to say, but when family is the 'only' thing keeping you in a place, it just doesn't seem like enough.

Although it is a huge part of your life, it may not be able to fulfill you in the way you are aching for. It's completely normal to want more and you can still love them at the same time.

I can't stand my hometown and have always wanted so much more out of life than staying there offered. That upsets the people I love who like where and how they live. It makes them feel like I'm making a judgment on their decisions by saying that isn't good enough for me. I get that.

But I know now that it doesn't make me wrong for feeling the way I do either. I refuse to make myself feel bad for having my own unique ideas, emotions, and dreams.

WHY YOU'RE NOT SELFISH FOR MOVING AWAY

Despite what others may think, I really don't believe it is selfish to want to seek out a more joyful life. Sometimes our current situation is holding us back or sometimes we feel like a change is key for shifting our mindset or perspective.

Whatever the reason, it is your life – you have to live with the consequences of your decisions. But parents especially tend to have a vested interest in those decisions.

Have you ever had your parents tell you about all the sacrifices they made for you – usually to remind you to be grateful? Many parents claim, *"I did this for you"* and tell you as you grow up that they want you to be happy and have plenty of opportunities for a good life to make their sacrifices worth it.

They just don't often imagine that may mean leaving to pursue a life far away and can feel betrayed when you decide to take off. However, the decision to become a parent and raise children was theirs, you never agreed to live on their terms just by the act of being born. Being grateful is a wonderful thing, but it isn't owed and can't be forced.

I'd never want to tell the people I love that I sacrificed my happiness for them. That is a horrible thing to put on someone, especially if the so-called sacrifice wasn't even a necessity. Of course, there are times when that kind of sacrifice is needed, but it should be done out of the kindness of your heart, not out of guilt, obligation, or as some way to use it against another person in the future.

I didn't want to look at my family and think '*I did this for you – I stayed here and wasted my life away in this town for you.*' Because, of course, they wouldn't realize the gravity of it all and there would be times when they canceled our plans or disappointed me, then I would be furious at their lack of appreciation. It would be inevitable. And it was unfair to put that kind of pressure on them to be the thing that was worth sacrificing our dreams and happiness for.

Luckily, our family and friends love us enough to let us go. And we love them enough to prioritize keeping in touch and making smaller sacrifices to make sure we are still part of their lives (like money or vacation time ... or talking on the phone for two hours even though we're exhausted).

We can joyfully show up for people because it is our own choice, and we aren't being guilted or coerced into it.

A few years ago, we met a man in Hawaii who was chosen as the cultural practitioner for his family at age five. He knew growing up that at some point he would be responsible for sharing the history of Hawaii on the small island of Molokai and accepted that role. But, as a young adult, he was encouraged to leave – to move away and build a life of his own. And he has now happily returned to take on the honor of his responsibility.

It didn't seem at all like something he was chained to and forced into. He could have decided not to come back, but because he had the option, it was an honor instead of an obligation.

I think this is how more families should handle their loved one's desire to move away. Make coming back an option that is encouraged and would be appreciated, instead of discouraging leaving or lashing out with anger when it is brought up.

REDEFINING LOVE

Here's the thing: claiming to love someone and becoming hateful when they don't want to do what you want them to is very contradictory. I just refuse to believe that trying to prevent someone from seeking out the things in this life that light up their soul is done out of love. It is based on fear.

Being afraid of losing someone and projecting that on them with guilt or threats is NOT an act of love.

Losing a close relationship with a family member or friend would hurt and that's scary. But love is being willing to push through that discomfort because you know the person who has your affection would be better off for it.

You are afraid of losing someone BECAUSE you love them, there's nothing wrong with that. But I don't believe constantly inflicting worries on someone about their safety or well-being is a healthy way to show love. It just feels suffocating and will probably drive them away or – worse – make them stay and be resentful.

Some people have their own issues (like abandonment or a need for control) that they project on others. I think this is a huge problem that can really prevent individuals who deal with this behavior from making big life decisions because they have unknowingly become enabling or codependent or manipulated.

So, say it with me: BOUNDARIES. Big ones. Everywhere.

You're going to need them if there are people in your life like this.

We all set our own value in relationships and have to communicate how we expect to be treated. You may need to use your move to start over with some people and build a new relationship with healthy boundaries and a different dynamic. Space really does help you do that.

However, making boundaries is easier said than done. Many people stay put out of fear or guilt created by the people who are supposed to love them most. And that breaks my heart. Love shouldn't feel like a weight holding you down, it should uplift you and fill you with joy.

Love, to me, is showing up. It's being able to be excited for someone else even when you aren't in a joyful place of your own. Realizing that makes us appreciate the people in our life who support us despite their own emotions or worries even more.

My best friend, who I've known since I was five, is the first to come to mind when I think of what love and support should look like from family and friends.

There was a time a few years ago that she called to tell me about some struggles she was having and, as she always does, she also asked how I was. Well, I had just had an amazing day swimming with wild dolphins in Hawaii – something she would love to do! So, I chose to just not mention it because it didn't feel like the right time.

When I told her about it a few days later, when she wasn't in a bad mood, she told me to never avoid telling her something I'm excited about just because she isn't having a good day.

She said, "knowing you had something amazing happen would have made me feel so much better." That big-hearted gem of a woman loves me so much that she could genuinely be happy for me, not jealous or annoyed, even though she was having a bad day.

That's love: being excited for someone because you find joy in their happiness, despite how you may be feeling. Love is not making someone feel like shit for being happy or seeking their own joy just because of personal feelings of sadness, jealousy, fear, or insecurity.

Moving away can bring up a lot of mixed emotions about the people you love and what you want out of this life. Guilt can really weigh on your heart at times and you can make yourself feel horribly selfish for chasing your own dreams.

But try not to. And when people show up for you in unexpected, beautiful ways, be sure to acknowledge that and do all you can to reciprocate.

MISSING VS. RESENTING

There is one downfall to those amazing supporters though – you are going to miss them like crazy!

However, one of the best lessons I've learned is to not let missing people be a bad thing. It is GOOD that you have people to miss. Acknowledge that.

Cry the tears when you need to. But please don't sit around feeling guilty or selfish if you have no real reason to.

If you choose to leave, it is almost inevitable that there will be a few people you miss. However, this is leaps and bounds better than staying and resenting the people who pushed you to do so.

Maybe some of the anger certain loved ones show is based on jealousy because they'd like to move also. Once you are settled in, they may consider following you or making a move of their own. Or they may just never be in a personal or financial situation to make that happen.

We know some people whose loved ones did end up following after visiting and falling in love with the new place or lifestyle as well – or maybe they just missed the person who moved enough to go for it. But definitely don't hold out false hope for this to happen. And if this isn't something you want, be sure to be honest about that if the conversation ever comes up.

While there are people we miss daily, we also are very open about liking to do life on our own terms. Unless it was a very special situation, most people would be disappointed if they moved to be close to us because we are always off doing our own thing. Being honest about that has been important to not give anyone unrealistic ideas.

HOW TO BREAK THE NEWS

With this whole moving away thing, how you and your loved ones communicate and express your emotions will really determine how well it goes. My best tip is to try your hardest to remain calm and logical. If feelings of anger, resentment, fear, or guilt start to build, try to identify why that is happening and work through those issues in a healthy way. And encourage loved ones to do the same.

While some people wait until their moving plans are finalized to 'rip off the band-aid' and break the news, others make their loved ones aware as soon as the idea starts to form by discussing a potential move even years in advance.

As a couple, we always talked about our desire to move and, even before that, I had been openly sharing that goal with everyone I knew my entire life. While we did kind of abruptly finalize our move to Colorado, we mentioned our desire to move pretty early on to start officially preparing everyone.

It can especially help most parents to have as much information as you can offer about how this new area will provide you with a safe, stable, happy place to live. Or, if that isn't necessarily the case, how you plan to manage it.

While sharing worries may come naturally depending on your relationship, be sure to focus on the exciting, happy aspects mostly – so not to worry them.

If feasible, start planning when you will visit them or vice versa before your move, so they have something to look forward to. That way, when you do move, you can say something like, 'see you in six months', which is a whole lot better than simply 'goodbye.'

Most importantly, don't act guilty for pursuing your dream and don't just put the whole thing on your spouse (for example, 'we have to leave for their job, dream, etc.'). Try to remain united and confident for best results. But also, be prepared for the inevitable flood of emotions coming your way no matter how well you handle breaking the news.

While some sadness is normal, you shouldn't have to be the recipient of hateful backlash. In all likelihood, you didn't make any promise to be around the corner forever, you didn't abandon someone who you had committed to help, and you didn't run away from caring for someone who was your responsibility.

You aren't some villain out to ruin lives or steal joy. You just decided to move away.

Questions to Ask Yourself

Is whatever guilt you are feeling self-inflicted or pushed on you?

Are there any resentments from others about your move?

Who are the most and least supportive people in your life?

Which people do you usually find yourself missing the most?

Is there anyone you should have better boundaries with?

Do you think you'd be able to stay (or move back) without becoming resentful?

How Relationships Change

When we left Florida, I barely saw my best friend. We've known each other since kindergarten and, somewhere along the way, started to take each other for granted.

I actually went back for another friend's bachelorette the year after I moved and purposely didn't even bother to tell her. She, of course, found out I was there and was upset she missed a chance to see me – we were still friends, after all.

But, at the time, I just didn't feel close to her anymore and didn't see the point of going out of my way to make it happen.

Yea. Ouch. (It should be noted that I have some DEEP trust issues and tend to build fast walls if someone disappoints me – but that's for another book.).

Fast forward to seven years later, when I literally crossed the world just to go back and be there for the birth of her first baby before leaving the country again.

And the year before that when I spent more than a month there helping her wrap up the final touches of her wedding day. I sobbed giving my matron of honor speech, because my love for that woman has grown into something so overwhelmingly special – so much richer and deeper and more honest than it ever could have if our friendship hadn't been tested.

Moving away is probably the single best thing I could have done for that relationship. It made us have tough conversations about the part we both played in letting our friendship start to die out and how important it was to us not to let that happen.

We rebuilt our trust, respect, and love for each other in a way we were never able to before.

Maybe we would have rekindled our connection if I had stayed. Maybe the credit should be given to just growing up and being more mature. But I think it would have been all too easy to put off that coffee date just one more week or that difficult call another day. (*And, let's be honest ... neither of us is all THAT mature*).

Not being physically present and available forces you to make an effort because you realize that person will only be in your life if you *both* make it happen. But note the emphasis on both ...

Of course, she wasn't the only friend I moved away from. Leaving town has been a clear way to figure out who is closest to me.

Sometimes it is the people you think it will be – like the family who basically adopted us when we lived in Colorado. Other times, the people you find yourself missing will take you by surprise – like the work colleague turned friend I've become much closer to

AFTER moving because I realized how much I missed our chats. There's even a couple we house sat for briefly in Hawaii who have become dear friends because they just made a permanent place in our hearts.

While I don't recommend moving just to figure out who your true friends are, it is a good perk! Plus, it helps you to prioritize your time much better.

QUALITY TIME

After moving, planning trips home was initially extremely stressful. I felt guilted into doing so much I didn't want to.

People who we hadn't seen for years would come out of the woodwork to say they wanted to see us. Which is flattering, but also extremely difficult to try to manage. Eventually, I realized that I was in complete control of the situation and had to be the one to set some ground rules.

There didn't have to be any more obligatory meetups with certain old friends, just to be nice, when we knew we should cut ties. We had a great excuse – we live half a day or more away. And when we are back for a visit, we only have limited time. Plus, it was usually our 'vacation' time, so we wanted to do our best to actually enjoy it!

Once we started to take more control over what our visits back to our hometown would be like, it became much better, and we even looked forward to it.

We've giggled on the bottom bunk of my nephew's bed as we whispered stories to each other after his bedtime, had family cooking nights, taken part in birthdays and other celebrations, spent all day watching movies or just doing life together with loved ones. I'm even known to go run errands with a few of my close girlfriends on their limited days off (and strangely love it so much!).

On longer visits, we have even taken off for a few days on our own for a top-secret mini-vacation we don't tell anyone else about. (Shhhh!)

Now, we make time for the people that are the most important to us by planning ahead with them. Our immediate family members and closest friends get the first pick of our time and for longer periods. Maybe we'll plan an entire weekend together or a day at the beach. (For example, we always make a point to try to hold Sunday lunches for Buddy's family, since that's their tradition).

Then everyone else has to put in some kind of effort. Gone are the days where we drive all over town trying to hug everyone. We'll make some exceptions for friends with kids or who have limited funds, but otherwise, we expect people to meet halfway.

Seeing that people will indeed make that effort is really encouraging! They even fully understand our need to prioritize family time and never try to make us feel bad about it.

And for those who don't make the effort? Eventually, we'll stop reaching out because it begins to seem pointless.

However, we've learned to never close a door completely. People can surprise you. And it is a wonderful thing when they do.

Of course, having loved ones visit you in your new home is especially fun because you can focus all your time on each other. If that's ever an option, we highly recommend it!

We've spent a week taking our nephew out exploring in Colorado where he saw snow and mountains and elk for the first time (and I had to hide my tears of joy, so I didn't lose any cool points!). Laughed as my dad let his fear of heights show on a mountain pass with no rails. Splashed around on paddleboards with my BFF and her then-boyfriend (now hubby) in a lake. And we even had some very dedicated friends meet us all the way in Hawaii for an epic friendcation – they are now forever dubbed our 'travel besties.' Such cherished memories!

While some people have a permanent place in your life, no matter where your epic journey takes you, others are just meant to show up for a few chapters or eventually take a less-important role. In the end, it's up to you who you let contribute to portions of your story. I'd recommend making sure they have good things to add!

ADAPTING TO DIFFERENT OPINIONS

Since we lived in the same hometown until adulthood, we are fortunate to have some friends we've known for as long as we can remember. Many are still in our life – just not all in the same way they used to be.

I realized long ago that some people are only meant to be in your life for a season and it isn't realistic to try to hold onto them for longer. I've also realized that you can love someone while still making less space for them in your life due to the toxicity they bring with them.

People change with life experiences and so do relationships.

A parent or sibling you didn't get along with as a teenager could be your best supporter as an adult. A friend you looked up to and respected could make a choice that changes the course of their life for the worst and disrupts your opinion of them completely. That's just how it is.

Or maybe you're the one who changed and don't seem as fun to be around to them anymore because you no longer share the same interests.

Our opinions and choices change as we get older. That's a given. But I think this is increased if you move away or travel or do other activities that encourage taking on different perspectives. There are a lot of people we love who we don't agree with on politics or other important issues. Even our general outlook on life is completely different. It is exhausting to try to manage that at times.

I can also understand that it is hard for family and long-time friends to realize they don't really know you anymore. And for some, now that you aren't as much like them, that realization frustrates, upsets, or even scares them. You'll likely start to realize who in your life just doesn't quite get you when you bring up moving for the first time.

It is really difficult for some people to understand why something that makes them happy doesn't do it for you or why you would uproot your entire life to seek out something that doesn't interest them at all. They just can't relate and that can be really off-putting – it can even lead to some of that resentful, negative behavior I mentioned before. And if you change your mind on major beliefs you were raised with, it can be really upsetting for them and will likely be a major topic in arguments.

However, while you may choose a different path, you can still appreciate why your family and friends have chosen theirs – and doing so can help encourage them to return the gesture.

You don't have to be the same to love someone. It is completely possible to appreciate where you came from and remain emotionally connected to those 'roots' without letting it keep you from moving away to start your own unique life and form your own opinions.

It's a hard balance, but learning to just accept their differences gets easier with time – even though you don't value the same things anymore (or maybe you never did!). And I personally think space helps to ease that because you can have more control over your interactions.

Even with changed opinions, leaving doesn't have to mean abandoning all sense of familial ties. But we also aren't trees and THANKFULLY have the ability to move wherever we'd like.

SEEKING OUT LIKE-MINDED PEOPLE

One of the things we've loved the most about moving away is making a conscious effort to add new people in our life that really line up with our values and who have similar life goals. This isn't something you can do with family or life-long friends.

Being able to "date around" when making new friends in a new place is actually really exciting. Of course, we invite conversations to broaden our perspectives and ideas, but someone who may be great to chat with once or twice isn't necessarily a great friend match.

If you meet someone who isn't your cup of tea, you can usually easily let that connection fade away without any drama because they aren't your friend's sister's boyfriend who will be at every cookout until the end of time. It's nice to be able to have the ability to choose who you spend time with based on genuine feelings, not obligation.

Although, at times, our newer friends become the main focus as we build a community in a new place. Our friends from past homes are always in our hearts and we prioritize our relationships with them as well.

We've actually been able to grow even closer to friends by having more opportunities through our chosen lifestyle to talk about deeper topics and share dreams. Funny enough, a few friends that we thought we weren't all that aligned with anymore eventually made some major life changes to focus on similar things.

It really shouldn't be that surprising that we are drawn to people with the same underlying values. While we may not be on the exact same timeline, I think we're all trying to get to the same place!

Both new and old friendships bring so much value to our lives. Both have shaped who we are. We cherish them all even more so as our life and location changes. However, sometimes we just have a friend for a short time and that's okay, too.

While all of the people we've connected with in various ways have a place in our hearts, they won't always have a place in our life. We're fine with that. Because forcing it has never worked out for us in the past and timing isn't always right for every relationship to succeed.

TIME AWAY CAN HEAL

As I noted in the story at the beginning of this chapter, sometimes distance really does make the heart grow fonder.

It just has a way of simplifying things for you. Even people you do have those short connections with can start to be people you think of fondly as you miss their company more and more.

When we left our hometown, there were people I had become disappointed in, detached from, or even wrote off completely. But that space allowed healing. I realized we didn't have to agree or be similar or even talk often for me to care for them deeply. Some people I had hardened my heart toward became the ones I missed most.

Being away allowed me to gain a new perspective that I couldn't see when I was swimming in the ocean of drama daily. I forgave. I asked for forgiveness. I grew as a person and became a better friend, sister, auntie, daughter, and wife because of it.

There are still those exhausting conversations and unaligned values to deal with, but I can prepare my heart better now and not let it push me away.

Every family (every relationship for that matter!) has its issues and will be unbearably frustrating at times. But I think knowing you are not there full-time really does help you to manage issues better.

Whatever you do, just don't close your heart to the people you love even though they may disappoint you at times. Make boundaries when needed. Keep your distance as necessary. But if you love them, don't let that fade. Because it's a wonderful thing – even with all the drama it may bring.

And when you see them, hug them ... really hug them. They may be a big reason why you left, but it is likely that they will also be the reason you keep returning. Relationships are a complicated thing, but they are also one of the most beautiful parts of being alive.

Questions to Ask Yourself

Do you think any of your relationships could use a little space?

Are there any interests or hobbies you'd love to find someone who shares?

Who do you think would come visit you? Have you talked to them about it?

What friends or family members do you know, deep down, no longer have a big place in your life?

Which loved ones do you hope you remain close to?

Harsh Realities of a Life Away

To be completely transparent, my heart feels more and more split the longer we are away. Some months – or even years – I feel great about my decision to move away. But when it has been too long since our last visit or, like with the pandemic, we aren't sure when we will even be able to get back ... I start to feel very torn.

Sometimes it feels like my heart is not whole and will never be. I've felt this way often over the years – even before we left – since I always wanted to pack up and go. I have a deep love for many people back in the U.S., but I've grown to dislike not just my hometown, but my home country (*aside from Hawaii ... it's just special there*).

I have no interest in taking part in the materialism, success obsession, inward-focused, stress-inducing way of life that is so prominent there. I don't see it having anything for me. I don't want to be there. Especially now that I know I can live differently in other places.

But, then again, part of me really wants to be able to happily exist in my hometown, so I can drive my nephew to school and be silly with him while he is still young enough to partake. And bring my new-mom bestie coffee for no reason except to just have a hug and a chat. I want to have more beach walks with my dad while he is still healthy and able. I want to spend hours concocting vegan meal ideas with my big bro. And visit my mom, a few states away, to help her with house projects and crafts.

Sometimes, I just want to be close by ... just in case. Just because.

I just don't want to do it there. Nothing in me wants to go back for anything aside from my loved ones. It makes me sick even thinking of it. Especially now. Especially with our home country looking like it is on a fast train with diminishing tracks.

I can't reconcile these feelings. If I had enough money, I'd just move them all to be with me wherever I land.

My heart hurts to feel like I have to choose. Everything in me has always wanted to leave. Everything in me still wants to stay gone. I really just don't like it there. I feel so sucked into the things I worked to distance myself from whenever I go back. I feel myself change into someone I don't want to be. Someone I left behind purposefully.

Yet, I just yearn for that time with them, especially our nephews and new niece. I just want to put my arms around them and know that they feel my love. Not have to assume they do from afar. I want to know.

But this is the life I chose. Exactly what I wanted. Our loved ones have their own choices. We can't push them to follow our same path. It's not for everyone. We get that.

And our connection as a couple, our marriage, is so strong BECAUSE we left. Honestly, we do best in our own little bubble, but I can't just stop caring about the people outside of it.

I can feel the time tick on. I can see our nephews and other kiddos we love getting older – my friends leaning more into their own lives, our parents aging.

Will I see them again? Will I have time to make those memories I want to? Will I regret not returning sooner? Will something finally change in my heart or mind that allows me to stay for more than a few weeks at a time? Would they ever move to be near me?

I just don't know. And I hate that most of all. Kind of ironic for someone who chases the unknown ...

ADVICE FOR MAKING IT WORK

Chances are, you will feel similarly torn every now and then.

Chasing your dreams never comes without sacrifice, that's for sure. Just give yourself a lot of grace. Don't let your emotions take you down a rocky path that you can't get back from. Remember why you left and try not to create unrealistic images of the people you are missing.

If you moved back, would anything even be different than before? Probably not. So, try not to let yourself spiral and, instead, focus on the life you so desperately sought out and make a point to stay in touch with the ones you left behind the best that you can!

And maybe, if you are dreaming up some non-reality where you could have everyone you love in the same place, go ahead and let that play out for about two minutes. Cool. Glad we agree that's probably a full-on disaster that would lead to, you guessed it ... another move!

I know from experience that it can be especially hard when you haven't yet created a support system in the new place you have chosen to call home – or if you move too often to really make one. When I have my meltdowns over missing people, it is usually when we haven't had meaningful social interactions outside our bubble for a while.

My best advice for anyone who is determined to move away is to make a plan to feel at home as soon as possible, as well as realistic expectations for how often you'll return for a visit.

For many people, there is this mindset that *"you left, so it is up to you to visit."* And let me just tell you, it sucks. For many, saving for a trip to see us just isn't a priority or genuinely isn't financially possible. I get it. But ... it still sucks.

Making an effort to build new connections quickly – even if it is just a coffee date with a coworker or joining a local club or volunteering – can really take the sting out of missing your people.

When we moved to Colorado, we both got jobs in offices (even though we could have worked online) because we wanted to meet people. My husband joined a bowling league where he met two of the couples who we are still close to. One of them got us involved with an animal rescue and we fell in love with that kind community as well.

While traveling full-time, we became part of a few online communities that facilitate meetups or events. We will even connect with people through Instagram and go out of our way to hang out in person. We also do house sitting and farm stays to make personal connections while we travel.

Sometimes you have to get creative! Just be open to it and seek out those friendships. Eventually, you'll have some great memories with new friends between visits with the loved ones you miss.

ADDRESSING STRUGGLES WITH VISITING

As we mentioned, it is unlikely for loved ones to visit us, especially now that we are often abroad, and many don't even have passports. It is on us to make sure we see them.

If you have or are planning to move away, I'd be surprised if this wasn't the case as well. I actually have a cousin who would pack up his newborn baby and two toddlers to go visit family. To that I say, hell no. That is a nightmare. But he was the one who moved, and he felt guilty (and probably a little left out) if he didn't make trips back for holidays regularly.

There are plenty of problems with being the one who always has to go back, but here are the top three and how we've learned to manage them:

1. There's always a sacrifice.

After you move, you often have to choose whether to use your vacation time and savings to go visit family or for something that you would enjoy more.

This can make going back to your boring same-old, same-old hometown a begrudging task, even if you are excited to see loved ones. Especially in the first years away, because enough time hasn't passed to really feel nostalgic about places you left behind. And I'd bet in most cases, it feels far from a vacation.

2. Quality time (& rest) can be hard to get.

If you are like us, you have at least six to ten different groups of people who want to see you and spend some quality time with you when you go back to visit. If this isn't planned correctly, you can end up running all over town, giving everyone a few hours of your time, and ending each day exhausted and frustrated.

We've started visiting longer and planning visits around certain people, so we can get that beloved quality time. But it is inevitable that someone will get their feelings hurt that way.

We've just gotten better at not feeling too bad about it. *'Catch ya next time!'* is a phrase we've gotten used to saying.

This isn't to say we don't love everyone, but trying to make time for all of them in a few days makes us want to avoid return trips. So, for us, there has to be some kind of plan to avoid a hectic visit!

3. You'll probably feel left out.

Depending on how often you go back, you'll likely see or hear about big changes in the lives of your loved ones that they never thought to tell you about.

You'll be on the outside of inside jokes or family memories. Some people may even say things like, "*You just don't get it, you're not here.*" Most people don't mean to upset you, but it can sting more than you expect.

Of course, you are happy to see loved ones going on as usual without you. It would be awful to think they are all just sitting around crying over missing you.

But part of you wishes they saved a little bigger space for you in their lives. Some will. And it will feel amazing. Just don't expect it from everyone.

There are some wonderful benefits to moving away and chasing your dreams of a different life. But there is no such thing as a perfect life.

I'm sharing these downfalls so you can be mentally and emotionally prepared for some of the struggles that will likely come with a big move. It isn't to convince you not to go. Buddy and I are the last ones to do that!

But I do encourage you to have a plan for how to handle visits, which likely means some tough conversations about what that may look like from both sides.

Questions to Ask Yourself

Do you have a plan for budgeting trips back if visiting is important to you?

Are you prepared to use most – or all – of your vacation time on visits to see family/friends?

What will you do if there is an emergency crisis with a loved one?

Who would you stay with and who would be a top priority to see?

Is there a way you could help facilitate your family to visit you?

What kind of friendships do you want at this new stage in your life?

Being Scared & Doing It Anyway

A lot of people feel like leaving their hometown will hurt their relationships because their parents or friends will be mad at them, and they don't want to upset them.

However, deep down, I think the main reason for putting off moving away is fear rather than guilt. It's scary to think the people you rely on for support won't be there for you – especially if they aren't backing you up with such a big decision. Some of those people even do all they can to pile on the fear and guilt to try to make you stay.

There are definitely some valid worries about regret. *Will you regret it more if you stay and abandon your dreams or if you go and miss out on seeing the people you love?* However, I really don't think it has to be either/or.

You can find a way to pursue both – it just won't look exactly like you imagined. And if your family is threatening to disown you if you leave, I'd seriously consider how healthy that relationship is and if it is worth staying for!

I think many people who have reached out to me to discuss moving away also let the criticisms of loved ones amplify their own fears. Sure, it sucks if your parents or siblings or friends refuse to support a big life change you are excited to take on. *But are their reasons against it valid or are you just letting their negativity pull you down?*

Maybe part of you wonders if you will be able to make it out there on your own. Maybe you worry that you won't be able to make new friends or build the life you're dreaming of. Maybe you are buying into the version of yourself others have described of someone who isn't brave or strong or capable.

But maybe, just maybe, you will PROVE THEM WRONG!

WORST-CASE SCENARIO

Let's be honest here ... you could fail miserably! Yes, this is a real possibility.

Everything could go wrong. Then what? Most of the time you'd end up right back where you are ... with a deflated ego, I'm sure. But generally fine. You could get another job, find new roommates, eventually get back on track financially, and just laugh about your failed move one day down the road.

However, even if things worked out semi-well. Even if you just got a small fraction of the life you've dreamed up, *what would THAT do for you?* In my experience, it will likely boost your self-confidence, introduce you to new passions and interests, improve your relationships and allow you to make new ones, and challenge you to grow as a human in great ways.

While the word 'challenge' probably brings up some fearful tingles for you, it is also most likely what excited you about moving in the first place. Part of you is probably so eager to prove to yourself and everyone else that you can do it.

You are likely yearning for different experiences and opinions and ways of doing life. *You can ignore that voice telling you to go for it, but is that what you really want?*

I'll never forget when I experienced the magic of the first snow of the season after our move to Colorado and how dang proud of myself I was when I drove in the snow for the first time ... because I was terrified to do it.

I hate driving normally and now this slippery stuff was out to get me also! But I did it. And eventually, it became just part of my life. Aside from particularly bad weather, it wasn't scary anymore either.

Getting the chance to be proud of yourself for overcoming obstacles and pushing past your comfort zone is an amazing feeling. But just realize that it all starts with fear.

DEALING WITH FEAR

Being afraid is uncomfortable. Sometimes fear of the unknown can be debilitating in our culture that prioritizes stability and safety and routine. I think that is why so many people who love you try to push their ideas of safety on you. They are terrified of you going off into the scary world where they can't help you. *But really, how safe are you now in comparison? And what good is that doing you?*

My husband once told me that he always thought you just had to grow up, get a job, get married, and have kids. That was the recipe for life he was taught – along with many other people.

But it turns out, neither of us has any interest in having kids or a typical nine-to-five job. Really ... this whole "grown up" thing can pretty much take a hike, too.

Once we decided to do life on our own terms, our fears for the future were exchanged with excitement for what's next. And it stopped mattering what anyone else thought.

We don't worry about things like we used to, because we've proven to ourselves that we are more than capable of figuring it out. We are gritty and creative and determined. We've got this!

Looking back, I can say with all certainty that moving away is really what started that change in us.

Putting yourself in situations that scare you is how you grow and learn and realize just how brave you are. It's how confidence and self-esteem are built up.

To be completely transparent, I am fear-motivated as well, but in the other direction. I was terrified of getting stuck in my hometown or in a life not rich with experiences, adventures, and opportunities for personal growth. We were actually SO DANG EXCITED to be chasing our dreams that we didn't really start missing our people until about a year after our first big move.

If you are eager to move away as well, I definitely recommend making sure it is a feasible decision for you at this stage in your life. Maybe it isn't practical. But if it is, don't let your irrational fears – or especially anyone else's – be the thing that holds you back from chasing that dream. If anything, let it motivate you more!

Plus, it takes courage to pursue something new. You may be surprised to find out later on that your bravery motivated others to do brave things in their own lives and follow their own dreams. We've had so many family members, friends, and acquaintances say we've inspired them – just by living the life we dreamed of and unashamedly seeking that out.

That is THE BEST compliment.

You can always go back. And if you at least try, you'll likely go back with some valuable life lessons.

BUT, CAN YOU REALLY JUST GO BACK?

Okay. Okay. I realize saying you can just go back is much simpler than that would probably be in reality. Yes, there would likely be a huge cost to do so and probably some wasted money. Yes, you would probably need to accept help from family and friends to make it happen. But, in most situations, it is completely doable.

The truth is: very little probably changed back in your previous home. Your mom still has that guest room all made up that she'd be happy for you to stay in. Your best friend still gets brunch at that same spot once a month and would love your company.

Maybe a few people had babies, got married or divorced, or changed jobs or houses. But overall, you could slide right back in. There is still room for you, at least when it comes to physical space.

The big question is: have you changed too much to go back?

For us, this is a strong yes. We love seeing our family and friends back in the mainland U.S., but we don't have the same lifestyle anymore. Many of our personal beliefs are different now, and we would be bored out of our minds and super stressed out after a month. We know that without a doubt.

We could go back. We know they would welcome us. But we would feel like outsiders. I feel like a trapped animal when we are in Florida too long. If we moved back, it would be like trying to keep a feral cat from ever going outside to explore again. I'd long for other places daily.

Because we don't belong there anymore. Truthfully, I don't think we ever did. It's just the place we were born, not our home – not where we were ever meant to be long-term.

We've visited for multiple weeks at a time since becoming nomadic and have actually grown to enjoy those trips, but we need an out. Otherwise, we would start to panic a bit.

That's why we didn't go back at the beginning of the pandemic – even though everyone was saying travelers needed to 'go home' to their country of residence and hunker down somewhere safe.

Home to us is on the road and the idea of getting stuck in our hometown was much scarier than not knowing when we'd be able to leave New Zealand.

However, that's not the case for everyone. Not everyone dislikes the place they were born as much as we do. Man, do I wish I could feel that way!

Maybe you love your hometown and left because of a job opportunity or desire to see new things. Or maybe it took moving for you to realize how wonderful the place you grew up really is. For you, going back might feel like getting a warm hug at the end of a long day. It may indeed be the place you belong.

I'd be willing to bet that you know in your heart if that's true for you or not. And even so, it never hurts to go on a grand adventure somewhere else just to make sure, if that is something you're considering. At least, if you do decide to go back one day after seeking your own path, it will be because you genuinely missed it and not just out of unwarranted guilt or trying to meet someone else's expectations for your life.

Questions to Ask Yourself

What are your biggest fears and concerns about moving away?

What comments are other people making that deter you from the move?

Are these fears of yours and others reasonable or illogical?

On paper, is it feasible and realistic for you to be able to move?

What personal characteristics do you have that can help you succeed?

In what ways are you excited to grow and learn?

What's stopping you, really?

Becoming Yourself

There was a moment during our first year of international travel that I knew I had finally stepped into the woman I always wanted to be.

I was sitting on a ferry on the way back from a day trip to Morocco from southern Spain. That trip was a big milestone for me because it really pushed me out of a lot of my comfort zones, and I was actually really afraid of having to navigate such a different culture than I'm used to – even though we were only there for six hours.

I've always wanted to be this brave woman who does scary things, but I grew up being told to be afraid of the world. The unknown is dangerous. Strangers aren't to be trusted.

I have spent a lot of time battling that fear and being jealous of women who seem so fearless. But, on that trip, I realized I didn't have to stop being afraid to be brave. I was already being brave and had been for a while, because I wasn't letting those unrealistic fears keep me from pursuing my dreams and growing as a person.

All of the challenges I had overcome allowed me to be this woman I am extremely proud of. It is the most amazing gift I could have ever given myself. And I find so much joy in getting to share my epiphanies with others.

Knowing I have more insights and life advice to offer my nephew and other loved ones BECAUSE I moved away, makes all the sad moments and struggles so worth it.

While many travelers have shared this same realization, I do find it extra special that I also have gotten the unique opportunity to see my husband grow into his best self as well. The immense respect, trust, and admiration we have for each other has created the kind of bond I didn't even know was possible.

RELYING ON YOURSELF

We've both been pretty much in charge of ourselves and our own finances since we were sixteen, but we didn't actually live on our own until we moved to Colorado.

We always had roommates back in Florida. Then, all of a sudden, we were laying on some blankets and watching a movie from my laptop on the floor of our very first apartment that was all ours. We had only brought clothes, our cat, and some necessities, so we had nothing much to move in. But we felt so grown up and FREE! So amazingly free – to just rebuild a life the way we wanted.

We figured out so much that first year – budgeting better, cooking healthier, driving in snow, hiking up mountains, initiating new friendships, and lots more. I even flew by myself for the first time to surprise a friend! It was probably one of the best years either of us has ever had.

Eventually, all the newness became our routine, but man ... it was such an adventure to get there, and we grew so much in the most positive ways. And looking back, no one was there propping us up. WE DID IT. Us! On our own.

CHANGING FOR THE BETTER

As I've mentioned, moving away brings the chance to consider different perspectives and ways of doing things.

One of the first things we learned in Colorado is the importance of recycling. It might sound ridiculous, but we just weren't encouraged to do so in Florida. But there, everyone had recycling bins and used reusable bottles. Of course, we were all in – why wouldn't we be? We knew it was right, but just genuinely never thought much about it!

We also became so much more aware of the importance of being healthy, eating right, and exercising. Especially because we loved to hike, but would feel awful if we didn't do the work to stay in good shape between trekking up mountains.

Colorado changed us in a way we will always be grateful for. It opened our eyes to easy, yet important ways we could be better people. And we met friends who encouraged us to keep up these new habits, which just made it even more fun!

Even though we've been gone from Colorado for many years now, those changes stuck. And now we've just expanded on it by growing even further through travel.

We learned how simply we could live during our year in a motorhome. Started to believe that people are indeed generally good through our travels. Realized how responsible and capable we are as we committed to take care of other people's homes and pets as house sitters. Became more empathetic and aware of issues all around the world – and especially in our home country – that we had been blind to before. And, most recently, figured out just how resilient we are when we had to scramble to figure out how to ride out the pandemic in New Zealand.

Most importantly, through all of this, we have realized what truly brings us joy and peace, as well as what we are passionate about and what we'd rather not be part of. We are proud of who we are and what we've accomplished through our relentless faith that God would show up for us as we move from place to place and try new things.

For us, home stopped being a specific location long ago – it's just a place we feel safe, where there are friends to be made, and adventures to be had. Which for us, could be almost anywhere.

LIKING YOURSELF

Staying in that town I grew up in was suffocating my dreams and sense of adventure. And I could feel it as it was happening. If I had stayed in Florida, I think I would have turned into a grumpy, overweight alcoholic. I really do.

I just wasn't motivated at all there and felt really hopeless about the future. I had big dreams and not going for them really depressed me. I hated feeling stuck.

Leaving allowed me to have the space to grow into the person I always wanted to be and build the type of life I could be proud of. When I struggle with missing family and feeling selfish for not just being satisfied with the same type of life they are, I always go back to the question: *"Who would I be had I stayed?"* and I know without a doubt that I made the right decision.

I have learned so much that I have been able to impart on others and hope to share with the beloved little ones in our life one day as well. My insights about life, love, and the world are deep and meaningful. I have had the opportunity to intensely know who I am and what my strengths and weaknesses are. Without a doubt, all of that would have been impossible had I not left.

I like who I am. I'm still a work in progress, but I'm someone my nephew can be proud to call his Auntie. And his Uncle Buddy has grown into a pretty awesome guy too!

With all my heart, I wish that we could have become these people without having to miss out on so much of his life. But I honestly don't think we could have grown this much without forging our own path. And our marriage probably wouldn't be this strong if we hadn't taken off on our own to make a life we love together.

There was a moment I'll always remember on a trip to visit my favorite kiddo that really reinforced that moving was the right decision. My nephew and I were playing tag and he said, *"Even though you climb mountains, I'm still faster than you."*

And it hit me – I'm the Auntie who climbs mountains. I'm the one who has goals and dreams I'm not afraid to reach for. I have the type of marriage I only pray he can have one day – filled with adventures and so much laughter. It took work and sacrifice, but I'm really genuinely proud of who I am and the example I'm setting.

For me, becoming myself – that woman I always wanted to be – was a journey in every sense of the word and continues to be. Like most journeys, that often involves movement. But the cool thing is, I'm feeling more and more comfortable with stillness, which I think means all the hard personal work is really paying off.

No matter what it looks like for you, I hope you allow yourself to take that journey as well. I think it is all too easy to focus outward and distract ourselves to avoid the difficult personal work, but making choices to be better people has far more value than any outward success ever could.

Questions to Ask Yourself

What habits would you like to stop or take up?

Are you proud of the person you see in the mirror?

Do you feel like you'd benefit from meeting people with different perspectives?

Are you open to personal change and excited to lean into it, or scared of it?

If you are part of a couple, is your partner aligned as well?

Building Stronger Bonds as a Couple

For couples moving away for the first time together, it can be an amazing opportunity to bond like you never have before.

From the dreaming and planning to the actual setting up of a whole new life. It's this grand adventure that you get to share with your favorite person.

However, our family situations paired with being very independent at young ages, allowed our life as a couple to always be more centered on our relationship than our families. So that has probably made it much easier for us than people more embedded in family life.

Even still, before we made our move out of Florida, we had fallen into quite the rut. We both felt angry to still be stuck there, unmotivated to make the most of each day, and were likely on a path to one day kill each other out of sheer boredom. (*Never underestimate the dangers of boredom*).

We didn't have a bad relationship by any means, but we weren't on a good path for it to continue to grow and improve.

We've always been very aligned with our dreams and ideas, but it hasn't always been an instant thing – sometimes it has come after weeks of deep talks to realize we are actually on the same page, just looking at it slightly differently.

While a move can create tension for some couples, those who are aligned in their dreams and goals will often find it to be one of the most wonderful times in their relationship. We certainly did! Getting to see each other solve problems and being challenged to do life in a new way together gives a jolt of excitement to a relationship.

I had been living with Buddy for more than five years when we moved to Colorado from Florida. Moving brought out an entirely new side of him. He became more social and outdoorsy and DIY-inclined and so very confident. It was like my husband finally gave himself permission to be the best version of himself. And I already thought he was great, so imagine how fortunate I felt that he could get even better!

NOT A QUICK FIX

Don't get me wrong though, moving wasn't the magic fix for everything – and actually created new tension at times.

Changing your location isn't going to make you fall back in love or save your failing marriage. But, getting a new perspective, removing yourself from family drama, learning to really rely on each other, and having something new and exciting to look forward to CAN offer opportunities for a renewed or deepened connection.

Like any other time, maintaining a healthy relationship while moving away takes effort. Communication is always key in any relationship, but it is even more important when planning and undertaking a move. Be honest about your fears and struggles, so that you can address them together.

It can be especially difficult to leave a support system and feel extra pressure to be there in a new, more in-depth way for each other as you build your new life. I think it is an amazing way to get closer, but it can also bring on a lot of stress. It is particularly difficult if one of you finds a job or friends before the other. Try to be conscious of leaving your significant other out and find ways to build your individual networks while still creating a lifestyle that allows you both to connect deeply with each other.

Sometimes it is all too easy to get excited about something new and just assume your partner is feeling the same. Be sure to check-in and make sure they are happy as well. This may mean coming down from your high a bit to meet them where they are, but that's just what you have to do sometimes when you love someone.

It's far better to reach those joyful heights again together than be up there alone.

AN OPPORTUNITY TO SHOW UP

When we lived in a motorhome in the U.S. for a year, I was terrified of staying in those dark, creepy middle-of-nowhere Forest Service camping spots. But they were free, and we were on a budget. So, that was our best option a few times.

And, of course, my husband loved being out in the heart of nature like that, so I felt awful for hating it so much.

But, when it was time to go to sleep, Buddy would wrap his arms around me really tightly and just wait for me to fall asleep because he wanted to make me feel safe. And he did.

He runs really hot and can't fall asleep cuddled up like that, but happily sacrificed his comfort to make sure I was okay.

If you are the one who seems to need the extra help more often than not, it can make you feel like a drag on your partner when venturing into a new situation like a big move.

But just be open about it and remember that they fell in love with you knowing you are a flawed human, just like them. There are plenty of ways you help them when they are struggling – whether it is offering a confidence boost when needed, helping them through awkward social interactions, or just making them laugh when they are taking life too seriously.

We all have our own contributions and needs in a relationship. It's okay if they don't look exactly the same as the person you are doing life with. Just show up.

YOU'RE GOING TO HAVE TO TALK MORE

The key really is communication with all of this. When big life changes occur, having longer, more in-depth conversations are necessary to make sure you are on the same page as a couple. If life just goes on as usual, problems may arise, but there usually aren't dozens of important choices to make in a short period of time.

Deciding to move is going to bring a landslide of important decision-making your way. And that's if you can even get on the same page about moving in the first place!

Plenty of couples hit a wall when moving away is discussed – maybe because one is closer to their family and doesn't want to leave or has a great career or has no interest in uprooting.

It can be pretty impossible to successfully plan a move if both partners aren't in agreement.

So ... get there. Before you do anything else, sit down together and talk it out. If you do both want to move away, make sure your goals are aligned and you have the same ideas around budget and timeline.

When we decided to leave Colorado and try out full-time RVing, it was after about four months of not being on the same page.

We had taken a vacation from our corporate jobs and materialistic life to go to Iceland where we lived out of a campervan for two weeks. After that, something flipped on in me. I was done being in the hamster wheel. I wanted out. I wanted more.

But Buddy had built an amazing career for himself, was comfortable, and didn't see how disconnected with each other and the most important parts of life we had become due to chasing a worldly view of success.

We had one big fight about it that left us both sobbing. It was the first time in our marriage we just really butted heads. So, I let it go for a few weeks, then we sat down and compromised to prioritize travel more – rather than pursuing van life. And I just prayed his heart would change to align more with my desire to get out completely.

Eventually, it did. It didn't look exactly like I had imagined (turns out he wanted out deep down too and was just really afraid to go for it), but we compromised a little more and made it work in a motorhome instead of a tiny van.

And I'm so glad I didn't continue to force my ideas down his throat. I've always been so thankful that he pushed back when I initially said I wanted to sell everything and live tiny.

It made me respect him more and allowed us to learn some hard lessons about communication and understanding and patience (a REALLY difficult one for me)!

Figuring out what to do when we didn't agree – something that rarely happens for us – was an important learning opportunity as a couple. It's a lot easier to communicate when you are both excited about the same thing. But talking through a mismatch of dreams for your future is much more challenging.

After a big move (especially if that is into a motorhome, like our second move was), you'll likely be each other's only support – at least for a little while – so you may as well work on getting better at communicating now. And, *really, could that be the worst thing for your relationship?*

Questions to Ask Yourself

Do you both ACTUALLY want to move?

Are you and your significant other good at communicating?

Do you think you are on the same page regarding dreams and future plans?

How well do you handle stress and challenges together?

Being Far Away & Nomad Insights

If you are like me, your first move won't be your last and you'll end up getting further and further away from the place you were born.

It's all well and good to plan a move a few hours' drive or flight away. But what if you are headed to the other side of the country – or the world? What if the cost to get back is more than your monthly rent or mortgage?

That starts to escalate some of these fears and issues I've gone over so far.

MULTIPLE FLIGHTS AWAY

In 2020, we decided to focus our travels in Oceania. Prior to that, we were always a non-stop flight away in case of an emergency. From New Zealand, going back would be much more complicated. Of course, the pandemic intensified that. But, even before, we had discussed the reality of going further away and what that would realistically look like.

Moving across or out of the country can often mean multiple flight connections and an entire day or multiple days of travel. Not only does that make returning in case of an emergency an expensive hassle, it makes returning for visits or having visitors less likely.

The more expensive and long the trip is, the less likely you and most other people are to take it. That's especially the case if you only have a certain amount of time for vacation or holidays every year, if you have kids in school, or if you are on a limited budget.

While a move further away or abroad is an exciting adventure, it does make going back for special occasions or emergencies or just because more of a challenge.

THE PERILS OF TIME ZONE MATH

Not only is a far-off move a more expensive endeavor, it will also be more challenging to keep in touch depending on the time zone differences.

New Zealand is 16 hours ahead of most of our family who lives on the East Coast. When we first arrived, I was so jet-lagged and confused, I tried to convince Buddy they have different calendars on this side of the world because I couldn't wrap my brain around it being an entirely different day.

To keep my head from exploding, I just started telling people we were eight hours behind … but tomorrow. I don't know why, but this makes way more sense to me. (*You may have guessed; I didn't ace math in school*).

Anyway, the point is, being in a different time zone can be confusing and make it extra difficult to keep in touch when you are waking up when everyone you know is already in the middle of their day.

Granted, you can definitely make it work. Lucky for me, I set my own work schedule, so I can take a break to catch up with friends and family whenever I need to.

But if you are working nine to five with a huge time difference, it can feel impossible to find a good time. You'll definitely want to schedule catch-up calls with the people you want to remain close with.

Finding the right time to schedule a call may just require some creativity. For example, I know my dad wakes up extra early, so I can call him before I go to bed (around 10 p.m.) and he probably just finished his morning bike ride. (The man is #GOALS, I'm telling you).

It may take some trial and error as well as adjustments, but you can figure out a way to make it work. However, you may be a little frustrated at first, so try to give yourself some grace during the learning curve and prep your loved ones to be ready to do the same.

Oh! And put your phone on silent when you go to sleep! Someone is bound to forget about the time difference and call you in the middle of the night. You're welcome...

MISSING WHAT'S FAMILIAR

Keep in mind that time zones and long flights back to visit won't be the biggest difference when you make a far-off move. Depending on where you go, there may be cultural, language, weather, and day-to-day differences as well.

Make sure you do your research before making a big move and try your best to prepare for any major changes.

However, it can be fun to have little surprise differences to bring some unexpected excitement to your day – so, don't worry too much and just enjoy the journey!

For example, we had a great laugh learning from our British friends how to properly eat 'eggs and soldiers' after absolutely failing on our own. And there have been more than a few mix-ups due to language differences. It's all just part of the adventure.

And if you have a mom like mine, I'm sure she would be more than happy to send you a giant care package of anything you are really missing from back home!

WHEN YOU ALWAYS MOVE: NOMAD INSIGHTS

Getting used to a new culture is one thing, but what if your plan is to move around often? That can make life a little more interesting. As soon as you are used to one area, you are fumbling to figure out the language and culture of the next.

For some of us, that sounds perfect – but it does take some getting used to if you are coming from a more traditional life.

The term 'digital nomad' has become pretty well-known. Some may roll their eyes at it. Some may be intrigued by it. For us, it is a pretty accurate description of our life right now. We work online for companies in the U.S. while traveling the world and moving to different places regularly.

Although we never feel anything that resembles homelessness, we technically don't have a place to call home. There's just a storage unit in Colorado with about two boxes of things we really need to go deal with and a car we need to sell.

Our life is very strange to most who can't imagine a life so far from the traditional values of "settling down." Throw in that we are in our 30s and not just doing a gap year after college and the eyebrows tend to raise a bit more. But that's all quite comical to us at this point.

If you are considering nomad life, our best advice for beginners is to try to maintain some kind of routine that isn't place-specific. Whether it is a once-a-week pizza night, playing cards before bed, doing yoga in the mornings, or just finding a new book at a second-hand store every couple of weeks. These kinds of things can make you feel a sense of home wherever you go.

You may have to get creative depending on where you end up, especially if your go-to date night food isn't anywhere to be found ... but then it just turns into a fun challenge! And, at the end of the day, if you get somewhere and realize you don't like it all that much, you still have those go-to activities you enjoy and find value in to fall back on and keep you sane as you learn to adjust.

Funny enough, the more you move, the more you find that most places have plenty of similarities to what you are used to. It is still new enough to be fun and exciting, but also familiar enough to give you some unexpected comfort.

KEEPING CONNECTED AS NOMADS

For those wondering how the heck you manage to have relationships with no home to speak of and a habit of moving every couple of months, weeks, or even days, we have the answer. The big secret is ... you try a bit of everything!

There is no easy way to keep connected when you are always on the move. You are going to have to try. It is going to have to be a priority. And if you are lucky, your loved ones will meet you halfway.

My sister-in-law once told me we were the best people she knew at keeping in touch and it is one of the most meaningful compliments I ever received. Because I beat myself up over needing to do better all the time.

My nephew might not remember the visits and postcards and all the times we went out of our way (and budget) to show up for him, but she will. And I just have to hope she'll be the one to remind him if he ever doubts how much we care.

I will say, for littler kiddos, postcards or boxes of treats from far-off lands are always a hit. Just realize this can get expensive depending on the postage costs where you are.

Of course, phone and video calls, as well as text messages, are a preferred way to keep in touch for most people.

WhatsApp is a great data-based messaging and calling option while traveling internationally. We also recently upgraded to an international phone plan through GoogleFi. It isn't seamless, but it is nice to be able to text and call everyone as usual without having to always switch to WiFi or have a new SIM card in each country we visit.

But we have found that we need to schedule times to chat – whether it is just a note to ourselves to check-in or a planned phone date we coordinated with a loved one. Everyone we know has extremely busy lives, and we're often limited in our availability due to time zones. So, planning is key to not lose touch!

We also set calendar reminders for birthdays, holidays, and other special occasions. Our reminder is weeks in advance if we plan to send a card or gift, since it can take a while.

Although there are also plenty of online options out there, if you need something sent quickly.

JUST PUT YOURSELF OUT THERE

While keeping in touch will likely be a priority, don't forget that traveling to somewhere new is an amazing opportunity to connect with other people as well. Whether they are short-term friends or people you like enough to stay in contact with long-term, putting yourself out there in social situations can lead to some amazing experiences.

We have celebrated New Year's Eve with a wonderful family in Italy (grandma even splashed us with bubbly for good luck!), had deep conversations with fellow backpackers at hostels in New Zealand, went out dancing with other travelers all night in Santorini, and had dozens of great cookouts with strangers-turned-friends that we met while RVing. We cherish those memories, often more than the places we made them in!

And we have stayed connected with so many of the people we've met through our travels. During the pandemic, we had friends contacting us from all over the world to see where we are, make sure we are okay, and offer to help if we needed it.

I used to think the world was this scary place with more bad people than good. Man, was I so wrong.

However, if you aren't comfortable just strolling up and talking to strangers, it can really help to join Facebook groups, forums, and travel groups that help to facilitate meetups and connections. We've found so much value in being in like-minded groups because we know it is highly likely that we will get along.

We met one of our favorite couples by being part of the same RVing group. We went out of our way to visit with them a few years back, fell in deep friend love, and have only gotten closer since.

In that same group, I also made another close friend just by reaching out to chat one day. That turned into clocking dozens of hours on the phone before we even had a chance to meet in person. We just have SO MUCH in common, it was like finding a long-lost twin.

Another way we have made a lot of friends is through Instagram. Most of the aspects of social media just annoy me, but Instagram really is an ideal way to keep in contact with people. It is also a great way to meet new people, just be careful about it!

We met another couple we had an instant connection with because they were fellow full-time travelers who were interested in house sitting. They reached out to us with a few questions and when I looked at their profile, I realized we'd be in the city they were in within a few days. So, we met up and had the most amazing time with them in Slovakia!

We met another housesitting family we adore this way also, so it really is effective!

Trying out opportunities like housesitting, work exchanges, staying at backpacker hostels, and other ways of travel that involve interacting with locals and/or other travelers are also great for meeting new people – and saving a ton of money on accommodations! Win-win!

Questions to Ask Yourself

If you are planning to move far away, how much would it cost to fly back?

How often do you plan to budget a return trip?

What parts of your lifestyle now are you hoping to be able to continue?

Do you have a way to stay in contact with loved ones while away?

Are social connections an important part of your life?

What kind of people are you hoping to meet in new places?

Final Thoughts

If you move away from people and places you love to go chase your dreams, a part of you will likely always feel like it is missing no matter what you do. Because you'll be leaving a piece of your heart behind with them.

But if you stay put, you'll likely long for your dreams while you are with them and maybe even let that keep you from loving them the way you want to. It's a struggle.

However, if you are creative, you can work out a way to feel less torn. You can keep in touch from afar, share your experiences, visit often, and even offer to introduce them to the places you love as well! And along the way, if you are really lucky, you'll find even more people to miss.

We thought moving away would mean having fewer close relationships. It would be us against the world. But it has been quite the opposite. While moving away has certainly made us even closer, it has also strengthened relationships we had all but given up on, brought dozens of new cherished people into our lives, and allowed us to realize home is a feeling – not a place.

Moving away has taught us a lot, but one of the most beautiful lessons is that we have people worth going back for. (*And trust me, the pull to be gone is strong within us*).

We may have thought we were running away from a city we hated and difficult relationships, but we realized years later that it was actually what we were running toward that made all the difference. All the joy and peace and self-discovery and genuine human connection that came from the journey – that's what we craved. We just didn't know that when we packed our car to leave all those years ago.

Really, it was never actually about moving away at all, it was moving toward a life that allowed us to grow, learn, and be challenged for the better.

Our initial move was in hopes of finding our own place to call home, but we've realized since that we've always held that within us. I sincerely hope that whatever your reasons for moving away or deciding to stay, that you are able to find that peace as well.

And if you have read through this entire book hoping I'll be the one to tell you in plain language what the right decision is for your situation, you may be a little disappointed.

While I enjoy sharing my insights, I'm not one to tell others how to live their lives. You have to balance the risks and rewards, then decide on your own.

The thing is ... staying or leaving won't guarantee your happiness, health, and success or that of your loved ones. No one can predict the future and there will be struggles either way.

But I will say, if you are looking for that sign ... if you are hoping for an excuse, something to point to in order to back-up your decision to stay or go, maybe that's the only proof you need.

Before You Go: Practical Checklists

Even though this book has been focused heavily on the emotional side of moving away, it is still important to be practical about your move and make some more strategic plans before you take off. So, I thought it was important to offer a few logistical insights as well.

While each location and situation will differ, here are a few helpful checklists to make sure you are on the right track for planning your big move!

BEFORE MOVING CHECKLIST

Before deciding to move, it is smart to narrow down a few top locations you would want to go and assess which is the best fit. Or if you already have a place in mind, be sure to do more in-depth research.

• Consider the climate, culture, and what kind of recreational options would be available to you in this new location. Will you need to make any adjustments due to weather?

- Find out if jobs in your field of expertise are realistically available and if the pay would be on track with what you require. Make sure you don't need any additional or different certifications to work in that state or country. Also consider the commute.

- If you are in college or planning to attend, look into how much in-state tuition would be and if it would be possible for you to transfer, if that is necessary.

- For people with kids, look into the quality of schools in the area, cost of daycare, and family friendly activities available.

- If you have pets, check to make sure they don't need any specific licenses or testing prior to moving. Also check for any rules or restrictions based on breeds, etc. If you are moving abroad, you will likely have to put your pets in quarantine, so plan accordingly.

- If you want to have a small farm or raise chickens, start a business out of your home, or some other activity that is important to you, make sure your location would allow that.

- It is also a good idea to check out the crime rates and overall political landscape to make sure there are no red flags you will wish you didn't have to put up with later.

- Most importantly, especially for those on a budget, you'll need to research cost of living and other fees or expenses to make sure it makes sense financially.

FEES & EXPENSES TO ASSESS

While you can certainly figure things out as you go, we find that being mentally and financially prepared for a big move really helps to lessen your stress.

Here are some important things to look into:

- **Taxes & Fees:**

  ◦ State taxes
  ◦ Local/city taxes
  ◦ Oddball taxes, like freelance taxes

- **General Cost of Living:**

  ◦ Home or rental prices
  ◦ Property taxes and other related home fees
  ◦ Water, gas, electric, trash, recycling, other utilities
  ◦ Costs associated to healthcare, plus quality of care
  ◦ General prices for groceries, gyms, daycare, etc.

- **Transportation Costs:**

  ◦ Car registration fees, including emissions testing
  ◦ Vehicle insurance cost
  ◦ Gas prices
  ◦ Prices for public transportation options
  ◦ Additional vehicle needs, such as snow tires
  ◦ Other automobile fees, like road-use fees, etc.

MOVING AWAY CHECKLIST

• Plan a new post-move budget based on the research you did before deciding to move.

• Outline a timeline and process for your move. Will you drive or fly and how many days should you dedicate to the move? Do you need any help? Do you need to take time off work? Do you need to plan any pre-move trips to make arrangements?

• Arrange short-term lodging to stay when you first arrive while looking for long-term lodging. Or find a trusted company or friend in the area to help you select a place to live before you move there.

• Determine if it is worth shipping furniture and other large items or just repurchasing them when you get there. Then, make a plan to move your belongings accordingly.

• Consider downsizing to save yourself time, money, and hassle when moving.

• Confirm that you have your birth certificate and any other important documentation you would need to return to your home state or city to collect.

• If moving abroad, arrange for a Visa or other documentation you'll need.

• Make plans for how to transport your pets and get any necessary proof of vaccines, etc.

• Find out how long you will have after moving to get a new driver's license and establish residency, then plan accordingly with time off work and keep the associated fees in mind.

• Join Local Facebook Groups and find bloggers to get insights into living in the area.

• Arrange for mail to be sent to your new address (whenever you have it).

• Give your notice at your job if starting a new one after the move or work out details of becoming a remote employee from a new location.

• If you have kids, sign them up for daycare and/or enroll them in school and notify their current school they are leaving (if needed).

• Discuss plans for coming back to visit or having friends and family come visit you, if desired.

• Plan a going-away party if you want one. Or ask someone to host it! This big life event deserves a celebration – even if it is just a solo one.

If you plan it out right, once you get to your new chosen destination, you can just focus on getting settled in and enjoying your new scenery!

But don't forget to pause and enjoy the excitement of the journey while you are making your big transition.

Moving Away Resources

Google & Bloggers: When it comes to researching your move, Google will be your new best friend. You should be able to find almost anything you need to know through a quick search. If not, try contacting the local government through their website for assistance. Bloggers in that city, state, or region can also be a huge help to give you an idea of what living in that area is like. They will probably even be happy to answer a few specific questions if you have any.

Local Government: In addition to reaching out to the local government of your new home, also be sure to reach out to your current government to make sure you do everything you need to before leaving. For example, when we left Florida, we didn't realize we were supposed to tell the DMV we moved and re-registered our car until we got a penalty fee in the mail. Luckily, I was able to have it removed after I provided the necessary information (and some mild begging).

Options for Trying Out Locations: If you aren't sure where you want to move to, we highly recommend trying out pet sitting or a work exchange program to help narrow down the options. While sites like WorkAway and HelpX work pretty well for people who don't mind having someone else dictate their schedule, house sitting really is the best option overall.

Getting to live in someone else's house in the area you are considering moving is one of the most realistic views of that area you are going to get. There are multiple housesitting websites out there, but we've always used TrustedHousesitters.com because it has the best usability by far and includes international options.

Points Credit Cards: If you are planning to visit family often, having a credit card that offers travel rewards points can save you a lot of money in the long run. For example, the Chase Southwest Visa can be used to obtain a Companion Pass with Southwest Airlines that allows a designated companion to fly for free with you for up to two years. While other cards, like the Chase Sapphire Reserve, offer points that can be used for many things from flights with various different airlines to hotels or even purchases on Amazon.

Nomad-Specific Resources

• **TrailingAway.com:** This is the blog website where my husband and I share more tips on nomad life – including housesitting and RVing. Plus, we have tons of fun travel stories as well!

• **A Beginner's Guide to Living in an RV**: For those curious about living, working, and traveling full-time in an RV, our friend Alyssa Padgett literally wrote the book on it and we highly recommend it for helpful insights.

• **TrustedHousesitters**: As mentioned, this is our go-to website for housesitting opportunities – a great affordable way to test out an area OR travel full-time for pet lovers!

• **Housesitting Magazine**: For more insights into housesitting, including first-timer guides and stories from around the world, this publication is a great resource.

• **MyPostcard**: This website is a lifesaver for people like me who find it really important to send cards on birthdays and holidays. It is so difficult to remember to send out cards when traveling, especially in enough time for them to make it back to the other side of the world. This site lets you do it all online and usually only takes a few days to deliver them!

• **VPN**: We initially got a VPN through Nord to make sure our internet is secure as we travel around, but in all honesty, we mostly use it to watch Netflix movies and shows available in other countries.

• **Escapees Mail-Forwarding Service:** This is a great service that collects, scans, and forwards your mail for you. They also offer an option to set up your mailing address with them (which can even be used for your driver's license and tax documents). We've used it for multiple years.

Acknowledgements

This book would not have happened had it not been for the support of my husband Buddy. Period.

He encouraged me to write it, kept me accountable, read it over and over to help me make sure I included all the important points, then took on the formatting and marketing to keep me from feeling too overwhelmed.

I don't think anyone has ever believed in another person like this man believes in me. This first *Moving Away* book, and any others in my future, can be completely attributed to his support.

I'd also like to thank all of the people who commented on my blog posts about moving away or reached out to me with heartfelt letters of thanks for sharing my insights. While Buddy was the support, you were the inspiration. I wanted to offer you more because I knew I had so much additional information to share on this topic.

And, finally, thank you to the amazing network of friends and family who lift me up in so many ways. A few specific ones who really speak into my life are Julie, Kelley, and Mel – thank you for always making me feel empowered and inspiring me through your own lives.

A special thanks is also due to my amazingly talented friend Alyssa who went first on this path to self-publishing and happily shared so many insights as well as encouragement. Her self-publishing course was a lifesaver!

About the Author

When Brooke and her husband Buddy moved to Colorado from their North Florida hometown in 2012, they had no idea that they were actually boarding quite the emotional roller coaster. Moving away brings so many mixed emotions and difficult changes in relationship dynamics. However, more than anything, it allows for growth – if you let it.

Since that fateful move to Colorado, the Baums have also completely started over by moving into an RV for a year, followed by another big leap into a life of full-time travel as international house sitters, and next is a Hawaiian home base. Moving away has become a way of life for them and has led to many important epiphanies.

They share about their travels and insights on their blog, TrailingAway.com.

Although Brooke has always felt compelled to write, her initial chosen career was actually in the field of psychology. While that didn't quite pan out, she has held onto her keen interest in the deeper, more emotional aspects of life and is most passionate when writing about love, faith, friendship, and personal growth. *Moving Away* is her first book, but it certainly won't be her last. There's so much more to share!

Note from the Author: If you don't mind taking the time to write a review for this book on Amazon, we'd greatly appreciate it and would love to read your comments! Thanks so much!

Made in the USA
Monee, IL
23 May 2024